MW00655849

www.thegooderLIFe.com

LEARN HOW TO NAVIGATE LIFE
WITH PURPOSE TO BE SUCCESSFUL AND
SET YOURSELF APART FROM THE CROWD

THE GOODER LIFE
IN LAYMAN'S TERMS

KENDALL LAYMAN

ISBN: 978-1-95691-446-7

CONTENTS

Background of the Gooder Life. 1

Success 7

Life-Changing Moments 13

The Essential Attitudes 29

    Thankful 33

    Humble 35

    Respectful. 39

Building Block Principles 43

    Purpose. 46

    Listen 56

    Think 64

    Aware 71

    Choice. 77

    Finish 84

Conclusion. 93

DEDICATION

Many friends and family members have played an important role in my journey toward The Gooder Life. I am thankful for each of them.

Uncle Neil, you planted in my mind the idea of living The Gooder Life. You may not realize the impact you've had on my life, but you've always challenged me to think. I'm eternally grateful for that.

Arlin, you're a rock of a man in my eyes. You've always demonstrated strength and purpose as you weathered a storm that knocked the color from your world. My gratitude for you is so deep. You managed to live The Gooder Life and regain your colorful world.

To my children, Rebecca and David. You have probably taught me more than I taught you. You endured my ideas and stories for years with only minor groans. You've given me many reasons to live The Gooder Life. I love you, and I'm proud of the wonderful adults you have become.

Kathy, you've been by my side for almost forty years. You're as much a part of this book as I am. You are my sounding board, my accountability partner, and my best friend. We cry together and celebrate together. We are a part of each other, we are one. You make my life Gooder every day.

BACKGROUND OF THE GOODER LIFE

"The only person you should try to
be better than is the person you
were yesterday." Matty Mullins

I've always been told I'm a straight shooter by everyone who knows me. So, I'm taking a risk in telling you up front that there are no new principles in what I call The Gooder Life. Still, I think you will find these lessons presented in a fresh way that is simple to remember and follow. I am not a philosophical genius, and I do not have a PhD in human behavior. There are those who enjoy intense philosophical ideas, books, and conversations. And there are those that prefer a more practical approach. While I enjoy both, I tend to mostly fall into the latter group. Maybe my last name was prophetic, and I'm meant to put things into terms that are easily understood. I'm going to share with you, in Layman's terms, how to pursue The Gooder Life.

For as long as I can remember, my mother's family has gathered each year for my Granny's birthday in March and again between Thanksgiving and Christmas. We celebrated Granny's 100th birthday in 2020 with fanfare and a large party. All six of her children are alive, and by the time all the aunts, uncles, cousins, grandkids, spouses, and children get together, we are a big group. Years ago, Uncle Neil built a large home on the old family farm. That is where we usually meet.

In my early thirties, I arrived at one of these events and Uncle Neil greeted me with the typical, "How are you doing?" I told him I was doing okay. What he said next has stuck with me for years. He said, "There are only two kinds of days: good or gooder." This sort of response was typical from him. I've always considered him a wise man who hid his wisdom behind a Southern, country, Arkansas farmer personality. He's an educated man who has worked in high levels of business during his lifetime. He knew his phrase was grammatically incorrect. That's what made it unforgettable for me.

I have told this story countless times, and it usually draws a laugh. But people always remember "good or gooder." His short statement has had a long-lasting impact on me. Maybe after reading this book, it will do the same for you.

I didn't initially understand the depth of his "good or gooder" concept. I thought of it as a decision that I would make each morning as I got out of bed and started my day. Do I want to be good or gooder today? Or maybe it was a decision that was made countless times throughout the day. I spent a lot of time contemplating this idea. How can we think in terms of good or gooder on our worst days, during those tragic moments many of us face at some point?

I'm generally an optimistic person. I have always admired my uncle's optimistic outlook on life too, but I was conflicted over how these two options could be our only options. I've had days, and I'm sure you have too, when "good or gooder" were not realistic options. I've watched as friends and family members have navigated tragic periods in their lives where they have grieved, mourned, and struggled to make it through the day. How can someone choose between "good or gooder" during those times?

Uncle Neil's words turned over and over in my mind as I tried to understand their meaning.

Was I to decide that each day would be no less than good? On my darkest days, could I find the goodness? Could I find a gooder day? Was it possible to encourage a friend to have a "good" day when something precious had just been snatched from them? I struggled to see how that kind of encouragement would be compassionate while someone was grieving.

But with time, the concept started to become clear to me. It's not necessarily a choice of one over the other. Instead, it's an attitude, a state of mind, a way of life.

The idea of The Gooder Life grew from that simple seed that Uncle Neil planted in my mind years ago. I'd been living The Gooder Life for years without knowing it. The practices and ideas I lived with, and often thought about, quickly fit together to create this vision and way of life. A way of life that simply encourages you to be better today than you were yesterday.

This book is for the student, the mother, the college graduate, the executive, the production worker, the athlete. If you are striving for more in your life, then this message is for you. The Gooder Life takes effort and discipline. It will not always be easy. It is rewarding. It will set you apart from the crowd. It will lead you to success. It will make you GOODER.

I wanted to come up with a logo, a visual representation to represent The Gooder Life. Doing so wasn't easy. I struggled with what type of graphic would properly convey this concept. At first, I pictured a road, which might illustrate movement in a certain direction. But The Gooder Life is not limited to one direction or path. I then considered designs that would indicate a journey, and while The Gooder Life is a journey, that idea didn't fit either.

I finally settled on a compass. A compass is an instrument that has been used for centuries by explorers, sailors, and many others to indicate direction. It's served as a lifeline for those who were lost and needed to find their way home. In the middle of a storm, it has been a comfort to many while helping them find a path to safety. For the Gooder Life, it represents movement, direction, and a way to ensure you continue in the direction you have chosen. Since a circle consists of 360 degrees, I think we can theoretically conclude that a compass has 360 degrees of direction. No single path works for everyone. We are all on our own journey. When you are living the Gooder Life, you don't necessarily need to be concerned with which direction you are moving. Instead, you must simply be concerned with moving, so your life doesn't become stagnant. Don't move backwards and don't stay where you are; that is the key. You are the one who gets to choose what each day will look like. Make your choices wisely. Live for right now.

The beauty of the Gooder Life is that you challenge yourself to be better each day. There isn't a prescribed amount of movement that must be accomplished each day. You may have days with massive growth spurts, or days with only tiny steps. The world can sometimes leave you feeling stripped of free will, but the Gooder Life will reestablish your sense of freedom. The Gooder Life will allow you to be you, a better you, the best you!

Throughout the book, you'll notice I have included questions at the end of several sections. I strongly encourage you to pause, think about what you have just read, and write down your answers. I don't want this to be a book that you read and then put on a shelf and forget about forever. I want you to seriously consider incorporating these principals into your life. My hope is that after writing down your answers, you will be able to easily thumb back through the book to refer to what you have written. Reading your own words will give you quick reminders for aspects of living the Gooder Life.

SUCCESS

"Success isn't overnight. It's when every
day you get a little better than before. It
adds up." Dwayne "The Rock" Johnson

Will you be successful? If you truly live The Gooder Life, then you absolutely will be. But you must first understand what success is. How can I promise you success if you live a Gooder Life? Well, what I deem real success may be different than what you normally consider.

What do you think of when you hear that word, success? Do you picture the CEO of a company? Someone who makes or appears to make tons of money? Someone famous? The word conjures up similar ideas in everyone's minds. While I am not saying those types of people aren't successful, it is important to understand that there are many people who aren't in those positions who are very successful.

In Earl Nightingale's book *The Strangest Secret*, he defines success the following way: "Success is the schoolteacher who's teaching school because that's what he or she wants to do. Success is the woman who's a wife and mother because she wanted to become a wife and mother and is doing a good job of it. Success is the man who runs the corner gas station because that was his dream, that's what he wanted to do. Success is the successful salesman who wants to become a top-notch salesman and grow and build with his organization. A success is anyone who is deliberately doing a predetermined job because that's what he or she decided to do deliberately."

I completely agree with Nightingale's definition, but I have noticed an ingredient that is prevalent in successful people that Mr. Nightingale did not point out in his book. Success is a result of purpose, and when the desire to serve others and build relationships drives that purpose, the outcome can be outstanding.

When we lived in Tucson, Arizona, we attended church with Cindy. Cindy was mentally handicapped, but that didn't stop her from having a purpose. She was at church whenever the doors were open. She was a favorite to many of us because her genuine happiness was contagious. Sometimes her parents would drop her at church, other times she would ride her bike since she didn't live far from the campus. She also worked at a nearby McDonalds and always smiled for her customers. Cindy was happy to serve, whether that meant singing in the choir or wiping down a table.

Cindy was successful. Why? Because she found purpose in what she did. Going to church to serve with friends and smiling for each customer at her day job fulfilled her sense of purpose.

The secret ingredient to Cindy's success was that she wanted to serve others. If you had met her, you would have seen that she loved other people as much as she loved herself. In Cindy's simple way, she built relationships with those around her.

Some people who know my wife probably wouldn't consider her successful in terms of money or status. She was a stay-at-home mom when our children were young. She worked for years as a volunteer at their schools, was a substitute teacher, classroom facilitator, and school secretary. Later, she worked for our local Chamber of Commerce. I assure you she did not become financially successful at any of these jobs. However, I consider her a success due to all the work she has done, from raising our children to helping serve the local community. She has fulfilled these poetic words from Ralph Waldo Emerson, the same ones that have been framed and hanging above her home desk for years:

"To laugh often and much;
To win the respect of intelligent people
and the affection of children;
To earn the appreciation of honest critics
and endure the betrayal of false friends;
To appreciate beauty,
To find the best in others;
To leave the world a bit better,
Whether by a healthy child, a garden
patch, or a redeemed social condition;
To know even one life has breathed
easier because you have lived.
This is to have succeeded"

There is so much purpose behind all the work Kathy has done, and that work always involved serving others and building relationships. That's why I can confidently call her a huge success.

Stan is my boss, mentor, and friend. He grew up in Alabama and graduated from Auburn University. He started his career as a service technician in the poultry industry and is currently the president of our company. He checks off all the boxes of traditional success.

One day, I decided to ask Stan for his take on his own success. I inquired about how he had gone from being a small-town kid to the president of a company. "What made you successful?" I asked. He told me that, early in his career, he had written three things on a piece of paper that he wanted to achieve. Two of them were material possessions, which he said lost importance to him after a few years. The third and last item on his list was to become the leader of a company.

I pressed him for the reason he had made that his goal. He said he simply wanted to lead people, build relationships, and create a team with the best people he could find. People who were good at the work they did. He wasn't after the title or the fame or the money. Relationship building and people, those are Stan's personal core values. He is focused on serving others every day. His concern for people goes hand in hand with the decisions he makes for our business, and those qualities have allowed him to realize his goal.

Stan then looked at me and asked, "Why are you successful?" I'd never been asked that question before, so I had to think for a minute before answering. Eventually, I told him I had not set out to be a leader in a company, but for most of my career I have been in leadership positions, and I enjoy being in those positions. Like Stan, I have never been interested in position or titles. I enjoy building relationships and serving others. When I finished telling Stan that, he looked at me and said, "That is why you are successful."

Now you know why I can say you will be successful. I'm not promising that living a Gooder Life will make you rich and famous, or that you will become the president of a company. But you might become those things. If you live your life doing what you set out to do, and you do it to the absolute best of your ability while focusing on serving others and building lasting relationships, you will find real success. Understanding that will change your perspective on your own success. And your success is probably the only thing you need to be concerned with. Don't let the opinions of others control you—it's what you think about yourself that matters.

LIFE-CHANGING MOMENTS

"There is no normal life that is free
of pain. It's the very wrestling with
our problems that can be the impetus
for our growth." Fred Rogers

As I grow older and reflect on my life, I forget many of the small details and instead focus on specific events to mark the time that's passed. I think everyone is probably the same way. These events might be good or bad or indifferent, but the point is that we skip from event to event when telling our life's story. I think of a big shot I made in a basketball game, a drama production I acted in, a camp I attended, a girl I once dated, the woman I married, my first job. You get the idea. Each event helps shape who we become. More specifically, how we respond to those events helps shape our lives. Some events hold more weight than others, but they're all important.

My job has allowed me to travel all around the world, which means a lot of time spent sitting in airports. A few years ago, I was waiting on a plane in Brazil and listening to a podcast when I was introduced to a man named Don Yeager. Don is an American sports journalist, author, and motivational speaker.

On this podcast, he was talking about his friend, Warrick Dunn. Warrick grew up in Louisiana as the oldest of six brothers and sisters. He went on to play football for Florida State University before being drafted by the Tampa Bay Buccaneers of the National Football League. When Warrick was eighteen, his mother—who was a police officer in Baton Rouge, Louisiana—was shot and killed while on duty.

Warrick was devastated. He had to take over as the man of the house and still fulfill his commitment to Florida State. During his first year in the NFL,

Warrick started a foundation that helps to provide homes for single mothers. He called it "Homes for the Holidays."

On this podcast, Don described the day Warrick met the man who murdered his mother. Warrick had asked Don to accompany him to the prison that day. Don explained all the particulars of the visit to the prison, but the part of the story that stood out to me was what happened after the visit. Don told Warrick how amazed he was that Warrick could go talk with that man in prison and remain so graceful. Warrick responded by saying, "There are those times in life where you will wake up and see the world differently. My mother used to tell me that adversity can make you bitter or better, and she always encouraged her children to be better."

When life-changing events occur, we wake up the next morning and see the world differently, and then we have a choice to make. We can take that event and either become bitter or better because of it. Warrick Dunn chose better. He chose to move forward. He allowed his "see the world differently" moment to drive him toward betterment.

Not all life-changing moments involve tragedy. Some events are filled with joy. Kathy and I are the grandparents of two little boys. One is five years old and the other is only a few months old. They have changed and fulfilled us in ways we never could've imagined. Having them enter our lives were wonderful, life-changing moments. Watching our grandchildren grow and learn gives us a new perspective on many things around us.

When Kathy and I got married—over 36 years ago—it was a happy day and a life-changing moment for each of us. We began melding our separate lives into one as a couple. We've had many joyous, impactful occasions over the years.

But one event, more so than any other, impacted the lives of our family forever.

My small hometown in Northwest Arkansas had one stoplight and a couple of 4-way stops. There were a variety of locally owned businesses that met most of our needs. Some of the shops that lined the main street were the five and dime, dry cleaner's, grocer's, dry goods store, automotive supply, the bank, and the print shop.

It was a safe little place with a population of approximately 1500 people. I could ride my bike all over town without my parents having to worry. When I was young, during summer breaks from school, I would wake up in the morning after mom and dad had already gone to work. I would immediately get on my bicycle and ride the half mile downtown to the newspaper office where my dad was employed as a printer. I never ate breakfast before my short ride, and upon arrival at the shop my dad would give me a dollar for breakfast. I would walk down main street to the grocery store where I would purchase a Hostess pastry and a small carton of milk. I would usually hang around the print shop until morning break time. Then my dad and I would walk across the street to the Farmers and Merchants Bank where my mom was employed as a teller. The bank had an old Coke machine in the breakroom, the kind where the Coke bottles were suspended from a rack and hung down in chilled water. My dad would put a quarter in the machine, and I would slide the bottle down the rack and pull it out. I was always afraid I would drop the bottle just as I was pulling it out. I loved sitting in the break room with my dad and mom and other adults. I'd sit there and listen to all their "grown-up" talk. That was always a highlight of my day.

Like most of the town residents, we were a lower middle-class family who lived a simple life. My family could be found at the Baptist church on Sunday mornings and most Sunday evenings. Mom and dad both sang in the choir and helped in the nursery. When I became a youth in the church, I especially enjoyed the "rap sessions" our youth director Bill facilitated on Wednesday evenings. He would throw out a bible verse, an idea, or a question, and debate would quickly break out among us teens. His format frustrated me sometimes because he would never tell us what he thought or give us the answers to any of his questions. There were times where we would leave the session to go home before we'd agreed upon any sort of answer. My mind would be churning for hours, even days, searching for the answers to what we'd discussed. He made us think on our own until we'd each formed independent conclusions.

Becky was my older sister, four years my senior. I was the little brother who loved to tag along with her and her friends. It annoyed her friends sometimes, but she was soft-hearted and had a hard time resisting my pleas to accompany them on their adventures. She was an all-American kind of girl: nice, funny, pretty with long blonde hair. She started piano lessons at a young age and diligently practiced until she was quite good. She was smart and studied to achieve excellent grades. During her college years, she worked as a volunteer with the Special Olympics. Dad, mom and I joined in with her and her volunteer work because that's the kind of family we were. If it was important to one of us, it was important to all of us. Becky graduated with a special education degree. She met Arlin, the love of her life, while pursuing her degree. They married soon after graduation.

As a teen, I played sports, made decent grades, and enjoyed school without ever getting into much trouble. But unlike Becky, I didn't know what I wanted to do after high school. She had her life planned out, and she followed that plan through to its fruition. I bounced around from a university to a handful of smaller colleges with a focus on the electronics field. Kathy and I married before either of us had finished college. After our first year of marriage, when I felt I wasn't getting anywhere in school, Kathy and I collectively decided I would join the U.S. Air Force. We knew it would lead to a job, and that I would be trained for a specific skill.

Electronics had been a passion of mine since childhood. It was not unusual to find me taking apart a piece of electronic equipment to see what was inside and trying my best to modify the components. It was only natural that I would pursue the electronics field when I entered college, and it made sense to continue that path when I entered the Air Force.

The electronics field is particularly reliant upon colors. Wires are color-coded, colored lines on resistors show their values, and there are various colored lights to almost every component. In college, I had always overcome my color blindness by asking another classmate or the instructor to help verify the color I thought I was looking at. I had learned to cope with my deficiency quite well—or at least I thought I had.

Kathy and I arrived in Little Rock, Arkansas very early one October morning for my initial physical to start the process of becoming a United States Air Force Airman. I had no idea the physical included a color blindness test. After the processing was completed for the physical, Kathy and I sat in a room awaiting my next instructions. Finally, an Air Force member called both of us into his office. He informed us that there was a problem with my examination because I had completely failed the color blindness test. This was unusual at these Air Force physicals, so he explained that they were going to administer a different type of test to make sure there wasn't a problem with the previous results. Again, I missed every question and failed the second color blindness test. After both test failures, I was informed that I would not be able to enter the Air Force as an electronics technician.

I was crushed. I didn't know what to do. The recruiter who gave us the news, sensing that we were disappointed, pulled out a three-ring binder that must have been six inches thick. The pages contained descriptions and requirements for each job the Air Force had. As he thumbed through the book, I distinctly remember him stopping on one page and asking if I would like to be a Food Service Technician. I asked him what that was, and he replied, "It's a cook." I replied, "I don't think so."

Then he came to a page that had two jobs on it: Computer Programmer and Computer Operator. I asked him what each of those were. He told me he wasn't quite sure, but there was a special test I would have to take, and I would have to achieve a passing score of at least 80% to get either job. He wasn't too encouraging—he told us only a miniscule percentage of people successfully passed.

By that point it was 3:00 p.m., and we had started our day at 4:00 a.m. I was exhausted, and now I was facing a two-hour logic test that few passed. Kathy and I discussed our options and decided I might as well give it a shot. To my surprise—and probably the recruiter's—I passed the test. Not knowing exactly what it was, I chose to become a Computer Operator.

While it was an honor to serve my country, I must admit that my main purpose for joining the Air Force was to receive training and learn skills that would lead to a civilian career. By August of 1987 I had completed my basic and technical training, and we were headed to Tucson, Arizona for my first Air Force assignment as a computer operator. On our way we stopped to visit Becky and Arlin in Tulsa, Oklahoma. They were expecting their first child in September. Knowing that we would not be there for the birth of their child, we wanted to spend some time with them and wish them well before we left. We enjoyed our overnight stay, and then we said our goodbyes the next morning.

Next, we made the long drive to the Sonoran Desert. The landscape fascinated us. I had never traveled very far outside of Northwest Arkansas, and the desert was quite a contrast to the tree-filled Ozark Mountains I was used to. I started my new duties at Davis-Monthan Air Force Base. We were getting settled into our apartment and learning to live in the hot, dry climate with cacti surrounding us.

On the morning of Sunday, September 6th, our phone rang. It was my sister. "Well, Ken, we have ourselves a baby boy," Becky said. This was 1987. We didn't have cell phones with cameras and video calls, so she described the baby to Kathy and me in detail and told us her childbirth story. We were excited and happy for them and wanted badly to be there to meet our little nephew.

Early the next morning, Monday, September 7th, my dad called to tell me that Becky was experiencing complications from her difficult labor. He explained that on Sunday evening, Arlin had gone from the hospital to their house to retrieve the things they needed to take the baby home. When he returned, he found Becky unresponsive in her room. She was given oxygen, which helped, but she couldn't keep her oxygen levels high enough on her own.

By Tuesday, the complications were significant enough that she was moved to the ICU. By that point, Kathy and I felt we needed to return to Tulsa to be with our family and help with the baby. We planned to only be in Tulsa for a week before returning to Tucson.

A few days after baby Ian was born, Arlin buckled him into his car seat and took him home while his mom was still in the ICU. Family members from both sides gathered in Tulsa, and we took shifts sitting at the hospital and then going to their house to take care of the baby and get some needed rest.

After a few days in the ICU, Becky was placed on a ventilator. The doctors were having trouble making progress with her condition. Every time they treated one symptom, another problem would arise. Her health had deteriorated to a point that on the evening of September 15th, nine days after Ian was born, it had become apparent that she would not live much longer.

News of her impending death spread quickly. The ICU waiting room filled with family and friends to standing room only. During the day on September 16th, the hospital staff moved the immediate family out of the crowded waiting room to a suite in the hospital, where we could wait and rest. The telephone in the suite was connected directly to the ICU. When the phone rang that afternoon, our hearts sank. We knew what the message on the other end of the line would be. Becky had fought hard to overcome the complications, but she had passed away.

During that moment, it seemed everything was spinning out of control. And at the same time it felt like the world had stopped. It was as if we were in this strange silent vacuum. I could not grasp what was happening or why it had happened. Our family had done everything right. We were good kids for our parents, we went to church every week, and Becky and Arlin had become a sweet family of their own. Becky was the mother of a 10-day-old baby. This couldn't happen to us. But it had.

When Arlin left the hospital to travel home on the evening of September 16th, he was the new father of a baby boy, and he was a 27-year-old widower. He had lost the love of his life. He had lost the dreams of their future together. Good was nowhere to be found. My parents returned to their home brokenhearted after losing their precious daughter. Good was nowhere to be found. After making the arrangements and attending the funeral, Kathy and I made the long, sad trip back to Tucson where the only people we had met were a few fellow airmen. Good was nowhere to be found.

Back in Tucson, we had no choice but to move on with our lives. But it felt as though we were only going through the motions. Our hearts were broken, and we were 1200 miles from home. 1200 miles from our heartbroken brother-in-law and our little nephew. It was extremely hard for both of us. My sister was gone, and I missed her terribly. Good was still very hard to find.

We're always told that "time heals all wounds", but I have learned that is not always true. Time gives us the opportunity to grieve and to learn how to live life with a broken heart. But time doesn't take away the wound. In 2018, Willie Nelson released a song entitled *Something You Get Through*. There is a line in the song that correctly explains, "It's not something you get over but it's something you get through." As time passed, Kathy and I began to meet more people and make new friends. We were learning how to get through. We would call home as much as possible, and we longed for those days when the mail would arrive with a VHS tape of our nephew, Ian. We would have given anything for FaceTime or Zoom back then.

So, how do we reconcile The Gooder Life when life deals a blow that makes even the smallest daily task difficult? The Gooder Life does not set a standard that says you must perform specified actions each day. There are no milestones or benchmarks that must be met. When you can do nothing else, The Gooder Life simply says: survive, lift your eyes, move. Kevin A. Thompson describes this idea perfectly in his blog post, *In Your Darkest Day, Survive and Advance*. He explains that there are times in life that are so dark it becomes hard to see your hand in front of your face. It's those times when getting out of bed is the most monumental task you have ever faced. Nothing requires you to be the pillar of strength for those around you. You do not have to be an example for everyone to follow. You simply need to survive that one day and advance to the next. This ideology pairs appropriately with the concept of The Gooder Life. Sometimes, being better today than you were yesterday means simply surviving. And that is okay. As I said before, The Gooder Life compass is there to show you that there is not a prescribed direction in which to move. Instead, you can choose from 360 degrees of direction. Your task is to just move in one of those directions.

For a long time after Becky's death, none of us would have been able to say we were good. And yet, Arlin found a way to survive and advance through his grief. Maybe he pushed forward because he knew a small life now depended on him. Or maybe he made a conscious decision to be better each day. Whatever it was driving him forward, I will forever be in awe of him. The determination he showed was remarkable. I will always be appreciative of the father he has been to my nephew all these years, and for the relationship that we still enjoy. After 28 years, Arlin found and married the second love of his life. He profoundly explained at a special family gathering that when Becky died, the color had been "knocked out of his life." I'm happy to say that life's color has finally returned for him.

Those grief-stricken days changed my life and will forever be a defining moment for me. Mark Twain said, "The two most important days in your life are the day you were born and the day you find out why." Becky's death and everything surrounding that time brought me to a point where my thinking changed. I suddenly had to know why I lived life the way I did. Why did I believe what I believed? Why did I say the things I said? I didn't want to go through the motions anymore, nor did I wish to do what other people said simply because it was "the way we've always done it." I wanted to ask questions that would take me out of my comfort zone and challenge the very foundations my life had been built upon. I wanted to know "why?"

and I didn't care where the answers took me. I've heard that life lessons truly begin at the edge of our comfort zone. I had certainly gone beyond the edge of my comfort zone, and I was ready to learn.

My life, as I now know, would not be the same following the gut-wrenching loss of my sister. It happened, and I didn't like it. But I'm thankful for what it has done for me. I know it may sound strange to hear that I'm thankful for such a tragic event, but without that life-changing moment I wouldn't know what I know now. I wouldn't be who I am. I wouldn't have what I have.

When I look back at my life before this event, I think of where I was living. Not my physical location, but in a more metaphorical and spiritual sense. I was just skimming life's surface. I was going through the motions of living, but it wasn't a deep living. My definition of deep living is digging down and finding out the truth behind all your actions.

I remember in the late '80s and early '90s, there were some pictures that became very popular. They were called autostereograms and were a type of abstract art. When you looked at the pictures on the surface, they didn't necessarily have a shape; they were just a bunch of shades of color. But if you looked into the colors and allowed your eyes to relax, a 3D image of an object would appear deep within the artwork.

Like those pictures, I wanted to take a deeper look at my actions, words, thoughts, and beliefs. I had to discover the truth behind those areas. It was scary to do that—I felt vulnerable because I was suddenly willing to walk away from everything I had built my life upon up until that point. I wanted a "real" life. I wanted truth at a level I had never known before.

As I said at the beginning of this chapter, not all life-changing moments are tragic. Certain moments might be extremely beneficial for you. The point is, you must take your moment, however tragic or joyous, and let it to be the motivation that drives you to a deeper way of life. I have learned that some of life's most beautiful lessons are born through pain, suffering, tragedy, and elation. It has been 34 years since Becky's passing, and my quest for truth is still ongoing. It has been very fulfilling but also frustrating at times. I want everyone around me to seek out this deepness, but I have learned on my journey that each person has their own truth-seeking timetable. I can't make them see what I have seen—they must move at their own pace. You're probably already taking a step in that direction, otherwise you wouldn't be reading this book.

What is your life-changing moment?

_____

_____

_____

Did you allow that moment to move you forward, backward, or did you become stagnant?

_____

_____

_____

If you have felt like a victim of your circumstances, what can you do to become the victor instead?

_____

_____

_____

THE ESSENTIAL ATTITUDES

"Do unto others as you would have others do unto you." Luke 6:31

There is a reason the verse above is called "The Golden Rule." The short simple phrase is an excellent reminder to measure our own actions, attitudes, and words. I took a business law class in college, and the professor stated at the very beginning of the class that if everyone would follow The Golden Rule, many of the laws we have now wouldn't be needed. He was right; we can't go wrong if we follow that advice.

Building is a great hobby of mine. I have built everything from small bookshelves to large houses. I love to work with my hands. In the building process, you learn very quickly that the foundation of a project is the key to its success. A bookshelf can have beautiful trim and even show good craftsmanship, but if the base is uneven it will always wobble. You can have a stunning house, but if the foundation underneath the house isn't solid it will crumble over time.

Many houses built today use concrete blocks as the base of the foundation. You can't stack the blocks on top of each other and expect them to support the weight of the structure on top of them. Mortar must be placed between the blocks to keep them in place and provide additional strength. When the hundreds of foundational blocks have been put in place with the connecting mortar, they become one solid structure.

We will examine The Gooder Life principles in the next few chapters. These principles, like concrete blocks, are important on their own. But when the essential attitudes, like mortar, are applied to them you will have a Gooder Life foundation that isn't easily shaken. Incorporating these attitudes and principles into your life will positively impact you and change the way you approach and think about everything. So, let's talk about essential attitudes. They are:

THANKFULNESS
HUMILITY
RESPECT

These attitudes are essential because they help shape our perspective about everything. Whether in a business setting or a personal setting, these attitudes are necessary for any relationship to be successful.

I have never met a truly successful person who did not reflect these attitudes. Please understand that I said "truly successful." If you've read my earlier chapter on success, you know what I mean. There are people who have ascended to high levels in their companies, who are making a lot of money and living in large homes. But they might not possess thankfulness, humility, or respect. Like it or not, the term "fake news" has recently become a part of our vocabulary. I like to say that these people are experiencing "fake success." Through the world's traditional lens, they are considered successful. But if we could hear what their employees or co-workers have to say about them, such a pretty picture might not be painted. We might tolerate their lack of gratitude, but overlooking arrogance and disrespect isn't as easy.

Most would agree that leaders should operate with honesty, integrity, and a variety of other traits. I do not disagree. But if one has respect for themselves and for others, honesty and integrity will fall beneath that umbrella of respect.

I am fortunate to have worked with many people who are thankful to be where they are. They are humbled to have had the opportunities they were given, and they respect and acknowledge the fact that they are surrounded by others who play key roles in helping them live up to the best of their abilities. I love working for and with these kinds of people. They are a joy to be around because they reflect the essentials of a Gooder Life.

On the other hand, I have met people who think they have achieved greatness. The world may even label them as successful, but if they are arrogant, insecure, disrespectful, or ungrateful, they will never experience true success and most definitely never live a Gooder Life. They are great in their own eyes, but they tend to be difficult to work with. People dread having to deal with them.

Think about the people you know who are humble, thankful, and respectful. Think about the people you know who are not. We can learn a lot from both groups.

THANKFUL

"Along my journey I have learned that
the more thankful I am, the more I
have to be thankful for." Unknown

Awareness and appreciation of our benefits in life is crucial for maintaining a thankful attitude. Although you have worked hard to be in your position, someone had to recognize your work for you to get where you are now. Be thankful for that recognition and for your ability to accomplish your work. All these aspects link together to give you what you have and get you where you are. Each aspect is worthy of your gratitude.

When our son was in high school, he was recruited to play football at a Division II college in Missouri. They offered him an athletic scholarship, but it wasn't enough money to cover his full tuition. We were told by the admissions staff that if his ACT score was one point higher, he would be able to access athletic scholarship money along with academic scholarship money. We bought materials that were guaranteed to help him increase his ACT score, and we paid for online ACT tutoring. Still, he fell one point short of the required score.

I had read an article that discussed how a thankful attitude had been shown to increase ACT scores. So, each night before bed, we encouraged David to write down three things he was thankful for. I told him that what he wrote down one night could not be repeated the next night. He diligently listed three things in his journal every night for several weeks, right up until the next testing date. To my surprise, and probably David's too, he raised his score on the next test. A grateful frame of mind was just what he needed. I don't understand all the scientific and psychological reasons for why this works, but it shows how our attitudes can make a difference.

We often get caught up in the frantic pace of life, and it becomes easy to take all the good stuff for granted. Let's face it: life is hard. You may be struggling with health, finances, job security, children, marital problems, or something else. You may feel like you should have a better position than the one you currently hold. You may need some practice to get into a mindset where being thankful is a more natural way of thinking for you. I encourage you to follow David's example by starting your own journal of gratitude. If you take this seriously, I'm certain you will gain a new perspective of your job and everything else in your life.

Look for the positives in your life. Celebrate the wins and be thankful for what you have. We have today; we can never go back to the past, and the future may never come. Enjoy the process of learning to live life now and living it with gratitude.

Start by jotting down three things you are thankful for today:

_____

_____

_____

HUMBLE

"It is always the secure who are humble." Gilbert Chesterton

We can reverse the above quote and say, "It is always the insecure who are arrogant." Not all insecure people are arrogant, but it seems that arrogant people must be insecure. Why else would they feel the need to boast about their accomplishments? Why do they crave compliments from others? I think insecurity forces them to need to make themselves out to be better than others.

I have started listening to podcasts quite regularly. I focus on broadcasts about teamwork, collaboration, living life to the fullest, being humble, and more. One podcast I particularly enjoy is *Insight with Gordon Mote*. Gordon is one of the most sought-after keyboard players in Nashville, Tennessee. He is extremely successful in his trade, and he is one of the most thankful, humble, and respectful persons I have ever heard talk. It's not surprising that his guests share many of the same qualities as Gordon.

One of his podcasts featured Bill Schnee, a Grammy and Emmy award-winning producer and engineer who has worked with some of the biggest musical acts in the world including Steely Dan, Chicago, Barbara Streisand, Amy Grant, George Harrison, and many more. He also worked with Whitney Houston on *The Bodyguard* soundtrack, which included the iconic song *I Will Always Love You*.

What I found most interesting while listening to Bill talk about his projects was that he expressed a genuine thankfulness for having the opportunities to work with world-renowned artists. He is world-renowned himself, but you would never know that from listening to him talk. He says that when he is engineering or producing a record, he looks at himself as a servant to the artist. He is there to serve their needs and wants. When someone has reached Bill's level in any industry and is willing to become a servant to others, they paint a perfect picture of humbleness.

I don't know either of these men personally, but I can tell from listening to them that Gordon Mote and Bill Schnee are as humble as they are because they are secure in their talents and abilities. They are thankful their talents have been recognized by others, and that they've had so many opportunities.

Being humble is closely tied to the previous essential attitude of being thankful. A thankful attitude allows a person to relax because they are secure in their current position in life, which in turn leads to a humble attitude. This is opposed to being insecure, which is where a person feels anxious and fearful about their current state in life. I have crossed paths with many people who have had nice jobs, lived in nice houses, and had nice families, yet they seemed to always be measuring themselves against a higher standard. I heard a saying years ago that is so true: if you are not living in a state of humbleness, life has a way of humbling you.

A former leader and CEO of the company I work for was one of the most humble leaders I have ever encountered. He regularly spoke to investors on Wall Street and was interviewed on national news programs. He never touted himself when the company achieved financial growth. Instead, he credited the team members who had put in the hard work. He also took full responsibility when there was decline and never blamed those who worked for him. He was not putting on a show for the cameras. It was how he led behind closed doors. He was confident in his abilities but never arrogant, and he appreciated his employees. My position in the company was several levels below his, yet if he saw me at the office or outside of work he would stop and talk as if we were old friends. He didn't do this for show; he did it because he respected every member of the company and was secure in who he was.

I currently oversee the Global Information Technology and Marketing operations for a research and development company. These two departments aren't the money-making arm of our business. We don't create the product we sell, and we don't handle our product each day like our production workers do. We play an important role supporting our business, but as a support entity, we actually cost the business money. So it is necessary that we find ways to add value to our company. We do that by striving to be servants.

In the IT department, we write programs and create processes to help the production departments carry out their day-to-day business. We train them to use the programs and applications we create. We promptly respond to anyone who needs help with those programs or their computers. We store and manage an enormous amount of data and work to ensure it is secure. Overall, we serve them so they may work as efficiently as possible.

Think about the role you play in your company or business. You may be the CEO or the janitor. The position doesn't matter, but your attitude to serve others does. Now, how can you serve the people you are around today?

_____

_____

_____

RESPECTFUL

*"How you make others feel
about themselves, says a lot
about you." Unknown*

We use the word respect when we talk about relationships, both personal and professional, at work, at school, and at home. But if you ask someone for their definition of respect, they might have to think for a while before answering.

Simplicity is best when trying to explain anything. Talkingtreebooks.com gives a simple definition for teaching children what respect means: "Respect is caring enough to consider how words and actions impact others. Having respect is when you feel good about someone because of how they act. Showing respect is when you care how your actions impact others."

Respect is a feeling we have for someone. We have respect for a co-worker who works hard every day, not for praise and glory, but because it is the right thing to do. We have respect for someone who is fighting a hard battle and does so with dignity. We have respect for elder generations because we realize they have more experience than us.

Showing respect is an action. We show respect by carefully choosing our words and actions when dealing with someone else. We understand we can negatively or positively impact anyone at any given time. We may have no reason to *have respect* for everyone we interact with. We may know nothing about the person, but we can and should *show respect* to everyone.

For a business to be successful its employees must have frank and candid conversations with each other. In the company I work at, family is one of our core values. Just like in any family, there are times when company team members disagree. Some of these disagreements become heated conversations or arguments. But they are needed at times and can be healthy if they are carried out with respect for everyone involved. For these frank disagreements to be healthy, it is imperative that everyone remains respectful and nothing becomes personal. It is critical that the conversation is centered around business matters only.

One day, in a meeting, a fellow manager in our company made a derogatory statement about one of the departments I lead. I was blindsided by the comment and could have confronted him on the spot, but I didn't. After the meeting, I approached my lead employees to gather facts about the matter. My gut reaction was confirmed. The comment that blindsided me had no merit, and I needed to set the record straight. This coworker and I have a friendly relationship, and I didn't want the problem to silently fester between us. I went to my colleague's office, and we had a private conversation about the matter. Initially, when I brought up the issue, we didn't see eye to eye, and it caused tension.

Neither of us said anything to the other that was a personal attack, though. We went over the facts and got to the core of the matter. We behaved reasonably and respectfully toward each other, which allowed our relationship to remain in good shape. This encounter ended on a positive note because of the respect we *had* for each other and *showed* each other.

Think about the people you encounter each day. Do you treat everyone with respect no matter their position? List specific ways you can show respect to the people you are around each day:

_____

_____

_____

BUILDING BLOCK PRINCIPLES

"Remember the importance of small actions. They're the building blocks in the architecture of your life, the quiet victories you win for yourself each day." Diane Dreher

I've watched leaders and employees, both good and bad, to find out what makes them the way they are. I've managed all types of employees and observed all types of people in the business world, and I've drawn some conclusions from my observations. What I've learned is that no matter the type or the size of a business, the qualities of successful people seem to always be the same. Even those outside of a business setting—the housewife, the stay-at-home mother, the coach, the athlete, the college student—all have these qualities if they are successful. They embody The Gooder Life essential attitudes and exhibit many of The Gooder Life principals. Here are the six main principles that I see people practice who are setting themselves apart from the crowd and are achieving success:

1. They have PURPOSE
2. They LISTEN
3. They THINK
4. They are AWARE
5. They make wise CHOICES
6. They FINISH

These building blocks create a strong foundation for people to be good leaders and employees, and they connect together with thankful, humble, and respectful attitudes. These principles and attitudes are foundational to someone seeking to live a Gooder Life. Of course, there are other important principles that help a person live a more positive life, but these six are crucial.

In order to live out these principles, we must consciously decide and be determined to practice them each day. The longer we practice them, the more natural they become. I don't know if we ever become perfect at exuding these principles, but if we seek to perfect them every day we can become proficient.

PURPOSE

"Find your purpose daily and live life to the fullest and never give up." M.D. Eger

Purpose is a key building block from which all other building blocks flow. It would be very difficult, if not impossible, to be a good listener if you have no purpose for listening. The same goes for thinking, being aware, making good choices, or finishing tasks. Having purpose keeps our path from veering off in too many directions and becoming crooked. Crooked paths take more of our time and energy to navigate.

We can become overwhelmed searching for grandiose reasons why we were placed on Earth. Some of us have a passion early on that drives us, while others search on and on without finding an answer for their life's purpose. Congratulations if you are one of those people who know what your purpose in life is. You can use that knowledge to ensure that all the things you do along the way are meaningful and are contributing toward your goal.

If you don't have a grasp on that bigger purpose, don't worry. There are hundreds of books written about finding purpose and living with that purpose. These can be helpful, but don't let yourself get too bogged down with all the different information. And don't work too hard to find it—it isn't top-secret information. Simply start by asking, "Who am I?" and "What am I here to do?" Maybe the most basic way to find purpose is by asking yourself this question: "What's important enough to me that I'm willing to trade my time for it?"

Don't worry about coming up with lofty answers. Keep it simple. This is personal, and only you can determine why you get out of bed and do what you do each day. Don't be indecisive when it comes to your purpose. You know what you need to do, so firmly set your sights on your goals and move toward them.

Our son always loved football. He dreamed of playing college football from the time he was a preschooler. That was his purpose and goal for a specific time during his life. Unfortunately, he was not given an unlimited supply of natural athletic ability. While he was in high school, I told him he would have to work harder than other players to make up for his lack of size, speed, and ability. He did work hard and put in extra time over several years. It resulted in him fulfilling that football dream. If you want to move beyond the norm and live a deeper and more fulfilling life, you'll likely have to dedicate some extra effort and time to set yourself apart from the crowd.

Jim Hensel—an author, motivational speaker, and mindset coach—was being interviewed on a podcast. He spoke about a scene in the Ridley Scott movie, *Gladiator*. In this scene, Emperor Commodus goes down to the Colosseum floor to meet the Gladiator, Maximus. Maximus was living as a slave. His family had been murdered, and he knew his life would end soon. Despite his imprisonment, when the emperor asked who he was, he answered with authority, "My name is Maximus Decimus Meridius, commander of the armies of the North, general of the Felix Legions, loyal servant to the true emperor Marcus Aurelius, father to a murdered son, husband to a murdered wife. And I will have my vengeance, in this life or the next." Maximus knew who he was. He knew what he was going to do. He had a purpose.

There are different areas of purpose. They include our life's purpose and our daily purpose. Let's say my life's purpose is being an airline pilot because I have a deep love of flying. That purpose will fulfill my passion, provide income for my family, and help other people physically get where they want to go. But I can't just decide to be a pilot. First, I must learn to fly a plane. I'll search for flight instructors in my area and set up flying lessons. I'll need to generate income to pay for the lessons and my normal living expenses while I'm training, so I'll need to find a job. Those things all have purpose because they contribute to my life's overall purpose. Most people probably think about those two areas when we hear the word purpose: the *big* purpose, and the purposeful *things* we do to achieve the *big* purpose. One important note is that our life's purpose may not always stay the same. Changes naturally occur over the course of a lifetime that may help or require our purpose to change, and that's okay.

Let's focus on all the small things we do in a day. When we go to the grocery store, we have a reason or purpose for going there. We usually have a list, and our mission is to purchase the items on the list. When we go out to mow the lawn, we have a mission or purpose, which is to cut the grass. Those examples are very simplistic, but the actions to accomplish them are the same in basic principle as for complex tasks. The more you ask yourself why you're doing a specific task, the more common it will be for you to know why you are doing what you're doing. That is how you gain purpose. It's about creating new habits. As Tom Ziglar has said, "Good habits are simply Purpose Producing Activities (PPA's) done every day."

You must know where you are going and why you are going there. You should know why you say what you say, why you read what you read, why you spend what you spend. You get the idea: you should identify the purpose behind all your actions and words.

It takes a little more effort and thought to live with purpose all the time. A purposeful life requires very intentional actions. One must actively interact and engage with every decision made, every word uttered, and every action performed. Life throws all kinds of craziness our way, but knowing your purpose helps keep you on the track you've determined for yourself.

In 1984, I was 19 years old and renting an apartment above a detached garage in Tulsa. I worked a full-time job during the day and went to school at night. I was a delivery driver for a photographic and printing supply house. It was a small, family-owned company with about a dozen employees. Our workday started at 8:00 a.m., so I would normally arrive at approximately 7:45 a.m., load my van, and be on my way for the morning deliveries. I distinctly remember one morning when an older gentleman who worked at the company took me aside and gave me some advice that I have followed ever since. He invited me to start coming in at 7:30 instead of 7:45 each day. That was a time when everyone got together, had a cup of coffee, discussed various things, and prepared for the day ahead. I followed his advice and started coming in earlier each day. What a difference it made.

I began to look forward to having morning coffee with the guys. The relaxed laughter was refreshing. The older men in the office would tell stories from their pasts that were entertaining. It was a great time to build relationships with my co-workers. Best of all, it gave me time to prepare for the day ahead. Instead of showing up at the last-minute then rushing to load my van and get away for the morning deliveries, I learned that 15 extra minutes each morning made a world of difference. Having this small chunk of additional time each morning helped me mentally prepare for the day.

Today, I usually arrive at my office about an hour before the workday begins. It's habit for me, but there are also reasons for my early arrival. First, it gives me time to complete any items that are easier completed in quiet before anyone else has arrived. Second, it lets me mentally prepare for the tasks that lie ahead the rest of the day. I think about the meetings I am going to have, and I consider my part in the meetings and the purpose of the meetings. I think about any conversations I plan to have that day, and I try to play out those conversations before they are had. Will everything happen exactly as I planned? Not always, but at least I have a general idea of what I am doing before I do it. Things will inevitably happen each day that were not on my calendar, or conversations will be had that were not planned. My mental preparation each day helps me prepare for spontaneity.

Organizing your thoughts, words, responses, and emotions before your day begins will give you an advantage because you will have already anticipated much of what will come your way. Your emotions will be under control because you will have worked through many possible scenarios. That puts you in the driver's seat without anyone else realizing it.

We may not always envision every scenario, but the goal is to be as prepared as possible before something happens. People too often engage in conversations without having any idea what they are going to say. This is a recipe for disaster. In many conversations, people will let their emotions control them. When that happens, there's no telling what will come out of someone's mouth. Do you know those times when you say something, then later, after you've had time to calm down, you wish you hadn't said it? Those are the times where emotions get out of control and take us somewhere we did not intend to go.

It's okay to stop and think for a moment before you reply to a question or a comment. We have been conditioned to think long, silent pauses in conversations are bad or uncomfortable. In reality, extended silence presents a great opportunity to think about what was just said, consider a response, or determine if a response is even necessary. If you get sidetracked by emotions or anything that takes you away from your purpose, stop and gather your thoughts before continuing. Know and stick to your purpose. Don't veer off the road, and don't let others steer you away from your purpose.

A few years ago, I was mentoring a young employee and we were discussing how to have talks with supervisors. My first piece of advice was to know the purpose of your conversation before engaging in it. Second, I told her to play out the conversation in her mind before it happened. By doing this, she could ensure that she would keep the conversation focused on relevant topics. All of us are busy, and most managers don't want to spend time on irrelevant discussions.

I had a conversation with Rebecca, our daughter, after her first semester of her freshman year in college. Like many freshmen students, she was struggling with learning how to manage class time, study time, work time, and sorority time without falling behind in any of those areas. Kathy and I felt it would be better if she came home and went to a local community college for at least a year before returning to the university where she'd started. I knew this would be a hard conversation because there would be strong emotions involved. I spent a lot of time mentally preparing how I thought the conversation would go. I envisioned all the possible reactions and responses I thought she might have. Making such an important change in her life could have led to a damaged relationship if I had handled it with my own initial feelings. Taking the time to carefully and logically prepare my words beforehand helped diffuse any emotions and allowed her to think through what would be best. That was our purpose. The conversation was emotional but in the end and to her credit, Rebecca handled it very maturely. Today, Rebecca is extremely successful in her career. I genuinely believe the conversation we had many years ago, and her ensuing move to a smaller college, contributed to her success.

I am a big fan of Steven Covey's book and course, *Seven Habits for Highly Effective People*. There is a section about proactive and reactive people. A reactive person is an emotional person. Something happens or something is said to them, and instead of thinking through their response, they just react. This often leads to trouble.

A proactive person will take time to consider what their response should be before they act or say something. They think and develop a purpose in their response. This thinking may occur in a split second, or it may be a longer period, but the point is that those who take the time to develop purpose behind their actions and words will be far more successful. I'll talk more about the proactive person later in the section on "Choice." My time spent mentally preparing each morning allows me to be more proactive than reactive.

There's a good chance that you have seen the following words, from the great Persian poet, Rumi, hanging on either a wall in a school or office building. They are a smart reminder for all of us and pertain to our words having purpose:

"Before you speak, let your words pass through three gates:

1. Is it true?
2. Is it necessary?
3. Is it kind?"

Our conversations should have purpose. We should speak intentionally and deliberately. If we practice letting our words pass through those three gates, we will find ourselves physically talking less but saying much more with the words we choose. The importance of what we say will increase, and the meaning of our words will be more substantial for those listening. On my desk at my office, I have written down a couple of prayers that I have adopted. The first is from legendary Alabama football coach Bear Bryant. The story goes that he kept a copy of this prayer in his wallet and would read or recite it to the Crimson Tide players. When I read this, it reminds me that all we have is right now, and that it is important to give myself fully and purposefully to each day:

"This is the beginning of a new day. God has given me this day to use as I will. I can waste it or use it for good. What I do today is very important because I am exchanging a day of my life for it. When tomorrow comes, this day will be gone forever, leaving something in its place I have traded for it. I want it to be gain, not loss—good, not evil. Success, not failure, in order that I shall not forget the price I paid for it." (Bear Bryant)

The second prayer I really appreciate forces me to focus on my purpose each day. Today is all I have, so I want to make it better for myself and those around me. This is from Amy Grant, a well-known singer and songwriter. The prayer is only two lines long and very simple at first glance, but to me it is profound and all encompassing:

> "Lord, lead me today to those I need and
> to those that need me, and let something
> I do have eternal significance."

A lot of people are "winging it" in life. They say and do things without giving their actions much, if any, thought. Be purposeful in everything you do and say. As the prayer above says, we are exchanging a piece of our lives for each day we live. Make sure the impression you leave today has significance and is a gooder part of your life.

What is your purpose today?

_____

_____

_____

What lasting value do you want your life's purpose to have?

_____

_____

_____

LISTEN

"We have two ears and one mouth
so that we can listen twice as
much as we speak." Epictetus

For many years, our company conducted an employee survey. Over and over, the chief complaint was that employees felt communication wasn't adequate. I imagine the results would be similar in most organizations. It's interesting to note that, no matter what program was put into place to try and improve communication, it would always be the chief complaint on the survey again the following year. Maybe because the effort to correct the problem was being placed in the wrong area. But more likely because people simply wanted to be listened to by their leaders.

If you look at the most common reasons why people divorce, you'll likely find poor communication or lack of communication on the list. On first thought, we may mistakenly think of communication only as talking. But there are two sides to it. Sharing information and expressing one's needs is one side while listening and actively trying to understand the information or needs is the other side. Some people don't share as much information as we may like, or they may have trouble clearly stating their needs. I've observed that the bigger problem we have is that we don't listen well.

I've never heard anyone complain that someone listens too much, but we can all think of someone who talks too much. Someone came to mind, didn't they? Conversations consist of both speaking and listening, but many times one participant dominates too much of the talking. Begin noticing your own listen-to-speak ratio; most of us need to work on it. It's important to respect the other person enough to invest yourself in the conversation by listening. Don't just "hear" what the other person is saying—listen and "learn" what they are saying.

A co-worker was involved in a meeting where his superior asked a question, and he explained his position. The next day, there was another meeting with the same participants. The leader asked the same question again. If this was a one-time event, we would assume that the person may have been distracted the previous day. But this was happening frequently with the same person in meetings. After a while, it was easy to conclude that the person was not listening, which quickly led to frustration. So, the employee may never effectively communicate with his superior because he realizes there is no listening occurring on the other end.

Another time, I was standing at the coffee bar at work having a casual conversation with a department director. He asked me a question, and after thinking over my response, I gave him my answer. We continued talking, and later in the conversation, he asked me the same question he had asked earlier. At this point, I realized he had not listened to my earlier response. He was looking at me and acknowledging that I was speaking to him, but he was not listening. Oh, he was *hearing* me—but he was not engaging with what I was saying.

Our preschool grandson doesn't always listen well, which can frustrate his parents. They are teaching him to listen. They try to capture his attention by having him maintain eye contact when they speak. They tell him to focus on their words. They are brief. They ask him to repeat what he heard. These are very basic techniques because he is young, but they are good lessons for all of us. Eliminating distractions, looking the speaker in the eye, and staying focused on what they are saying are good places to start.

Beyond that basic advice, we must realize that listening is about the person who is speaking—not about us. We have all been there. We start listening, but then we have an extremely important thought that we must immediately share. It just can't wait! We have to say it! We wait for a brief pause so we can interject. We are simply waiting to talk; that's not listening. Our mind becomes focused on what we want to say, and we take our focus off the speaker's words. We are waiting for a gap in the conversation so we can jump in with our two cents.

Sometimes we mistake quietness for listening. That isn't always the case. Someone may be quietly forming a response without hearing your words. I know I'm guilty of this at times. Below is a personal example I'm not proud of, but I'm telling you anyway so you can avoid making the same mistake.

One afternoon, I received a call from a friend who was going through a very tense and confusing time at work. They needed someone they could be completely honest with as they vented all their frustration. I felt honored that they trusted me enough to let me listen. However, while this team member was talking to me, I was busy thinking back to a time in my career that was very similar to the situation they were experiencing. When there was a pause in the conversation, I began to share my experience. Suddenly, I realized that this conversation was not about the experience I once had, it was about being a friend and listening. I was breaking my own listening rules. My story was relevant, but completely unnecessary. I had to remind myself this was not about me; it was about them.

Another factor involved in being a good listener is understanding that listening brings responsibility with it. Few people think about the role responsibility plays when we consider listening, but it's very important. Over time, I have built relationships with friends, family members, and colleagues who have proven to be trustworthy. Because of the bonds we've created, I feel comfortable sharing personal thoughts, feelings, and confidential business plans with them. When I share that information with someone, I am entrusting them with something important to me. I have often been involved in conversations where someone asks me to keep some information confidential. I take their request very seriously, as I believe it ties back to the essential attitude of respect. If I truly respect the person I am listening to, I will absolutely keep their information confidential.

Think about a time when you had a conversation with someone and shared information with them that you wanted to stay just between the two of you. However, to your surprise, you found out that your private information had been shared. First, that should tell you the person you were talking to wasn't very trustworthy. Second, that person you were talking to didn't respect you enough to listen responsibly. Choose wisely when deciding with whom you will share private information, and always be responsible with the information someone shares with you.

I've had the privilege of mentoring several people. Some I had known for a long time, while others I've hardly known. The first few conversations I'd have with these people revolved around getting to know each other and building a relationship where trust could be established. Many of the people I have mentored have been younger and somewhat early in their careers, while a few have been seasoned professionals. The younger ones are usually looking for help to navigate confusing situations in the workplace, or they want to know how to navigate the years that lie ahead of them. Sometimes the ones who have been around a while are struggling with something in their work life and want advice regarding how to overcome their current challenges. I have also had employees come to me and ask if I would be a sounding board for them. They wanted to air their frustrations or maybe get feedback on ideas. They needed a confidential safe place where they wouldn't be ridiculed or dismissed.

No matter the reason behind why I'm mentoring someone, it is more about me listening to them than me giving advice. Unfortunately, I've found that some mentors simply want to be talkers. They want to tell the mentee about their career, their accomplishments, and how they overcame obstacles. While all of that can be good information in some settings, being a mentor or a listener is not about you, it is about the person who is sharing the information.

The world is constantly bombarding us with sound. Televisions with 24-hour news cycles are on in many businesses and homes. Satellite radio plays in our cars while we drive. We wear earbuds when we walk, run, work, eat lunch, and shop. The noise makes it difficult to listen.

There comes a time when we need quiet. Sometimes we need to talk to someone, and we need them to listen. Being a good listener is another way you will set yourself apart from the crowd. If you can learn to be a good listener, you will be a rare commodity.

Are you a good listener? What would others say? Many people think they listen well, but they don't. Adam Grant, PhD, has written a book called *The Lost Art of Listening*. In it, he states, "It's common for doctors to interrupt their patients within 11 seconds, even though patients may need 29 seconds to describe their symptoms. And among managers who had been rated as the worst listeners by their employees, 94 percent of them evaluated themselves as good or very good listeners."

We must become better listeners. But how do we get better when it doesn't seem to come naturally to most of us? There are things we can do to overcome our deficiencies. Aletheia Luna, the renowned author, said, "Listening *is* an art. It requires us to be patient, receptive, open-minded, and non-judgmental. It requires us to not put words in other people's mouths, fill in gaps, or presume to understand the other person fully."

Who do you know that listens well? Are they a co-worker, friend, parent, or maybe your boss? Think about what makes them a good listener and follow their lead. Here's a summary of points to practice to become a better listener:

1. Eliminate distractions such as cell phones, smart watches, and other screens.
2. Look the speaker in the eye.
3. Resist the urge to make it about you.
4. Listen to learn.
5. Repeat what you think you heard.
6. Ask follow-up questions.
7. Respect the person you are listening to by being responsible with what you hear.

Who do you consider to be a good listener?

_____

_____

_____

Who was the last person you really listened to?

_____
_____
_____

What can you practice to become a better listener?

_____
_____
_____

THINK

"Thinking is the hardest work there
is, which is probably the reason why
so few engage in it." Henry Ford

Dr. Albert Schweitzer was being interviewed in London many years ago when a reporter asked, "Doctor, what's wrong with men today?" The doctor was silent, and then answered, "Men simply don't think." I believe his words are still true today. Not enough people think for themselves. In the previous section I talked about listening, and in this section I will discuss the ability to think. I like to refer to it as having "lost the art of thinking."

The world has taken people who have a public position—or people who are more persistent in what they say or are the loudest in what they say—and labeled them leaders in our society, even though many times they are not leaders at all. We have been conditioned to listen to these so-called leaders and take what they say as the unquestioned truth. No thinking required.

We've allowed calculators to take away the need to think about basic math. Autocorrection functions have taken away our need to think about spelling and grammar. Computer-generated ads are always on our screens, so we don't even have to think about what we want to buy. A few impulsive clicks, and a package is on its way.

In an earlier chapter on "Life Changing Moments," I mentioned the time Kathy and I were part of our church youth group and how our youth director, Bill, would make us think for ourselves. I remember being so frustrated with his methods. I would search for answers to the questions he would ask, and when I would proudly go to him with what I had found and ask if I was right, he would grin and say, "I don't know, you tell me." It would make me so mad, but now I'm so thankful for his answer. Bill was forcing us to think for ourselves

Thinking is more than having an opinion; it requires knowing the reason behind the opinion we have. What we think determines our attitude, our words, the choices we make, and the actions we perform.

Our present reality provides a great example of how experts have told us what we could do in our homes, what we could do outside of our homes, who we could associate with, what we had to wear when we were with others, how we could run our businesses, etc. We live in a world where pastors tell us their interpretation of the Bible, the media tell us what they want us to know, big tech leads us down certain paths on social media, and doctors and professors tell us about their areas of expertise. Everywhere we turn, there is an expert telling us something. The problem with this is that these experts rarely agree with one another. People end up taking a side that sounds the most reasonable in the moment instead of weighing all aspects and then forming a belief. We can examine all the opinions, conduct our own research, and make up our own minds about matters. We were given brains and the ability to think, and that is extremely powerful.

When my children were in junior high and high school, I would sometimes gather all of us together for family meetings. This was usually to address specific events in our lives at any given time. No matter what the subject of the meeting was, we would always encourage our kids to think for themselves and ask questions. When my children would approach me with a problem, I would always tell them, "There are no problems, there are only solutions." I wanted them to think past the issue to come up with ways to solve it. In a way, I passed on to my kids what Bill, our youth director, had given to me many years earlier: the encouragement to think for themselves.

Kathy and I love being grandparents to two beautiful young boys. Our grandson, who recently turned five, is extremely smart and full of questions. Many of his questions revolve around the question "why?" By asking "why?" he is building a repository of knowledge in his brain. One day, as I was watching him ask Rebecca, his mother, a series of questions, I thought about how sad it is that as we get older, we lose our "why?" Maybe we grow tired of asking over and over. Maybe as we get older, we are embarrassed to ask questions in a group setting. Maybe we think our questions are stupid. Whatever the reason, we need to learn how to regain our "why?" We are never too old to ask questions, and we are never too old to learn. The world, more than ever before, needs thinkers.

In Isaiah 1:18 from the Bible, there is a passage that says, "Come now, and let us reason together." Dictionary.com tells us that "to reason" means "to think or argue in a logical manner." Today, it seems like we have lost our ability to reason. We have become so timid that we avoid entering debates with each other in person, and instead we hide behind screen names and argue on social media using our keyboard as our mouthpiece. We have become so afraid that telling the truth might offend someone, oftentimes we will not tell the truth at all. Or we'll simply remain quiet. According to that verse in Isaiah, it is good to reason, to debate, to be challenged. When we are challenged, we are sometimes pushed outside of our comfort zone.

Notice that the dictionary instructs us to challenge in a logical manner. That's easier said than done, but sticking to the facts and leaving your emotions out of it helps. Being respectful is necessary if you wish to have constructive, crucial conversations. When an instructor or a person in a leadership position says something that we feel is incorrect or which we don't understand, we must question them in a respectful way. These methods won't be productive if you are approaching the situation as an opportunity to knock someone down or belittle them. You must be respectful and listen to learn.

If you are the one being questioned by someone, it's also crucial that you accept that questioning in a respectful, non-defensive way. Respect is one of the "essential attitudes" and is crucial for having fruitful discussions. We also must understand that just because we challenge or discuss something, it does not mean that we will convince the other party to join our point of view or that we will walk away in agreement. In fact, we won't always think the same way as others, and that's okay. It's about standing up for what you think. It's about learning something you need to know. It's about calling someone out when they are wrong. It's about creating stimulating discussion that may cause you or someone else to consider a new idea.

When children begin to color pictures, they are often told to stay within the lines because it's wrong to go outside of them. From an early age, we begin to teach our children to conform. Now, don't get me wrong, I understand the need for boundaries, especially in young people's lives. However, coloring outside a line is not "wrong." The picture may not be as pretty, but not allowing the color to go everywhere can dampen creativity. Do you know why we are told to think outside the box? Because we have been conditioned all our lives to think inside the box! We often feel we need permission to think this way, when we should be thinking like this all the time. Getting outside that box needs to become our norm. Getting outside the box causes us to think deeper, which in turn can bring about innovation and creativity.

I have already pointed out how inundated we are with noise in our society. Some of it is out of our control, but most of it is our own choice. I don't believe our brains were meant for the information overload we experience due to the 24-hour news cycle and bombardment from social media. It can become burdensome. Keeping up with it may even cause anxiety and depression for some. Reading and hearing so much information on so many topics all the time doesn't allow us to slow down and properly consider what we're learning. I strongly encourage you to turn everything off for determined periods of time so you can entertain thoughts one at a time.

Silence may be uncomfortable at first, but it is necessary to think. I can hear all the excuses now about how you think better with some noise or light music playing. Do me a favor—just give it a try. Practice silent thinking for brief periods. Then, slowly work your way to longer stretches. You may develop a new perspective.

Our brains are incredible. They allow us to think for ourselves. We don't always need experts telling us what to do or think about any given topic. We can weigh information and determine which pieces we can discard or which we should hold on to. This might mean you have to think a little harder to formulate your opinions, but that's part of living The Gooder Life. There is freedom in understanding that we decide what to think about, what we hear and what we read. Be a thinker and a reasoner. Step out of the box with your own thoughts and be confident and secure in what you believe. People are going to disagree with you, and sometimes they may have a valid point that you should consider. Always be willing to learn and adjust your thoughts as you grow. Become wiser, and don't let a multitude of opinions easily sway you.

Write down a time where you thought for yourself that didn't follow popular opinion:

_____

_____

_____

Think of a time when someone questioned your thinking. How did you receive their questioning? Did you become defensive, or did you allow it to help you better understand your position?

_____

_____

_____

AWARE

"Awareness requires living in the here
and now, and not in the elsewhere,
the past or the future." Eric Berne

I am a huge fan of the Jason Bourne movies starring Matt Damon. If you've seen these films, you know that when Jason Bourne walks into a room, he immediately knows what each person is doing. He knows where a threat might come from, his exit points, and most importantly, whether he is in a safe or dangerous setting. I understand these are fictional movies, but in our everyday lives, we must learn how to scan a room and understand our surroundings. We need to be more like Jason Bourne!

Chad Morris is a football coach who spent a couple of years as coach of the Arkansas Razorbacks. He didn't have much success during his time in Fayetteville, but he did say something that resonated with me. In one of the first team meetings with his players, he told them that they needed to "be where your feet are." That simply means to be engaged with your mind, body, and spirit wherever you are. Be aware of your current surroundings and don't physically be in one place while your mind is worrying about something somewhere else.

Have you ever been in a situation where someone says or does something that is completely inappropriate for that specific time or place?

THE GOODER LIFE IN LAYMAN'S TERMS

Maybe you've been in a meeting when someone brings up a subject or asks a question, and in your mind, you immediately know that it's not the time or place for that comment or question. Have you experienced that silent groan or internal eye roll? Then you already have some awareness. You were aware of the mood and understood it. I can't stress the importance of this enough. Awareness and humility are crucial to becoming a successful leader or employee.

Have you ever walked into a room and immediately sensed tension? That's your awareness. Having that allows you to say the right thing at the right time based on your understanding of a situation. Having awareness lets us know that we may need to hold back on saying something we had planned to discuss. If we aren't aware in these circumstances, we risk being annoying, being thought of as a nuisance, not being relevant, or having what we say be forgotten because it was simply the wrong place and time. The right words at the right moment are more important than you think.

It may take time for you to be able to read a room, but the sooner you start paying attention to the emotions and attitudes that are there, the sooner you will begin to sharpen your awareness skills. Observe faces and body language. Listen to the tone of voices and the words that are said—or not said. Are people joking with each other or being serious? Is the conversation solely centered around business or is there talk about an upcoming ballgame on the weekend? Even the literal temperature of a room can affect emotions.

If it is overly cold in a room, people might be stiffer. If it is warm, people might be more relaxed. It takes all our senses to read the emotions and feelings in a room. You can quickly sense frustration, boredom, stress, happiness, sadness, or excitement if you make the effort to pay attention.

Dr. Travis Bradberry is a well-known author and speaker on Emotional Intelligence. He says that emotions are present in everything we do, and it's how we handle our emotions and the emotions of others that will dictate our success. According to him, 90% of top performers in the workplace possess a high level of emotional intelligence.

Problems and opportunities often disrupt our lives, and we have been conditioned to allow those problems and opportunities to shape our emotions and make us feel a certain way. When we begin to realize that we control our own emotions through the choices we make, we will be well on our way to becoming more emotionally intelligent. No one controls how I feel except me.

While it is important to be aware of our surroundings, it is equally important to be aware of what is going on in other people's lives. I refer to this as social awareness. Everyone has a personal story, which you may or may not know. My wife was a high school secretary when our son was in high school. She was privy to very personal information about students, but she kept that information confidential. She understood that student behavior often had more to do with what was going on at home than it did with what was happening at school. Our son was sometimes quick to pass judgement on other kids, even some of his own friends, when he experienced negative interactions or witnessed bad behavior. I can't tell you how many times I heard Kathy tell him, "Give them a break. You never know what a person is dealing with."

People often fail to consider that a person has a life outside of what you see. When I was in the Air Force, I remember sitting in a non-commissioned officer class while the instructor was talking about this very subject. It was a class on leadership, and he was saying that, as leaders, we must understand that each person always has their own story. Maybe a new mother comes in late to work one day, and while she is there, she begins making mistakes that are not normal for her. She may have been up all night with a sick baby. The last thing we should do is chastise her for being late and making mistakes. Instead, we need to be aware that this behavior is not normal for her. There must be something going on with her personally that is contributing to these uncharacteristic actions. While lessened productivity or bad behavior can't always be excused, a person's personal story needs to be considered. And that doesn't necessarily mean that we need to know what their story is. We simply need to be mindful that they have a personal story.

Some time ago I had an employee who was uncharacteristically struggling with a poor attitude at work. The bad attitude had gotten to a point that executives in our company were asking me to do something about it. I knew the employee was struggling with life issues outside of work, and it was obvious that those issues were largely the reason for their attitude and suffering performance. One Friday afternoon, I had a conversation with the employee and told them I knew they had a lot going on outside of work, but that did not excuse their performance. Instead of punishing the employee, I asked them to go home, take some time over the weekend to clear their head, get their attitude adjusted, and then come back Monday with a fresh start. I had no idea what would happen on Monday when the employee came back. To their credit, they came back to work with a new perspective and a changed attitude.

When my father was diagnosed with cancer and it later became evident that a cure was not going to be found for him, there were days I went to work with a completely unfocused mind. I was thinking about what life was going to be like without my dad. I was obviously quite distracted. I'll always remember and value the compassionate treatment I received from my leaders at that time. They knew there was more going on in my life beyond work.

Practicing emotional awareness requires you to notice, feel, and evaluate the emotions of the people around you. Taking all of this into consideration and then considering our thoughts and words will allow us to say and do the right things at the right times. Being aware keeps us from sticking our foot in our mouth quite as often. Being aware is important if you want to set yourself apart from the crowd.

Think of ways you can improve your emotional IQ:

_____

_____

_____

Think of a time when you judged someone for their actions without knowing what was going on in their life. How could you have acted differently?

_____

_____

_____

CHOICE

"I am not a product of my
circumstances. I am a product of
my decisions." Stephen Covey

We start making choices as soon as we wake each morning. Liz Murray says, "The fork in the road happens over a hundred times a day, and it's the choices that you make that will determine the shape of your life." When our alarm clock goes off each morning, we decide whether to get out of bed or stay in bed. We don't always think about every choice we make throughout the day. Some of them seem automatic, and we don't even realize we've made a choice. But even the mundane things we do like drinking coffee, eating, brushing our teeth, or getting dressed are all choices.

Other choices aren't as simple. Some take time to analyze and are difficult to make. Deciding to take a new job or move cities means working through a list of pros and cons. Choosing to make a marriage proposal means considering the lifelong commitment you are promising another person. Other times, we are forced into quick decisions and must go with our initial gut instinct. Regardless of the situation, choices are important because they impact our lives.

Similar to Liz Murray's thoughts on choices, a friend often reminds me that we are the sum total of all our choices. That is a powerful, truthful statement. Stop for a moment and think back on your life. As you assess the choices you've made, you will notice how all those choices shaped you into who you are and influenced where you are. That thought could be uplifting or depressing depending on how good or poor your decisions have been.

Stephen Covey's book *The Seven Habits of Highly Effective People* made a huge impact on the way I live. His ideas are so important that I bought the teen version for each of my children when they were younger. The topics he covered were regularly taught and discussed in our home. I even managed to reference some of the ideas during my toast to the bride and groom at our daughter's wedding. The looks Rebecca gave her brother during my speech were priceless. I knew exactly what they were saying in their heads, "Here goes dad again, talking about the seven habits."

In Covey's book, the first habit is to be proactive. Being proactive means that we have the capacity to choose our response. "What response?" you ask. Your response to everything! The one area that we have absolute control over is our ability to choose. We choose how we think. We choose how we react to situations. We choose our attitude. We choose our feelings. That is powerful! Many of us aren't convinced that our feelings are our choice. It's not an easy concept to grasp because it takes realizing that our happiness and anger are within our control. We choose to be happy or not. We choose to be angry. As much as we like to blame those two emotions on our circumstances or on others, they are ultimately our choice. Like most things, it takes practice to become good at reminding ourselves of this and choosing well.

Sometimes the good choices we make don't result in the easiest roads to travel. Extra effort will be required, but it is incredible how small bursts of extra effort will set you apart from other people. In *The Strangest Secret*, Nightingale also tells us why it only takes small efforts to look different: because most people conform to the norms of society. Doing what everyone else is doing—and doing it that way because that is the way it has always been done—will simply make you blend in with the crowd. Mr. Nightingale says that only one out of twenty people truly set their sights on what they want to do in life and then give the necessary extra effort to go and do it. While I can't verify Mr. Nightingale's number, I do know that choosing to be different, and giving the effort it takes to be better today than you were yesterday, will set you apart from the crowd.

Chris Rubio is a former starting long snapper for the UCLA Bruins football team. During his three years as the starter, he never had a bad snap. Not one. Now he holds instructional camps around the country every year and coaches hundreds of high school long snappers into college scholarship-worthy players. Chris tells his football students, "You have to do what others won't to achieve what others don't." He stresses the importance of being disciplined in every movement necessary to snap the ball to the punter and being willing to practice more than your opponent. No matter what you are involved in—whether it's school, sports, family, or your career—you will have opportunities to separate yourself from the crowd. Will you choose to give the extra effort, to go the extra mile and stand out? Or will you conform to doing what everyone else is doing? It's your choice.

For many, the global pandemic has been a life-changing moment. There are countless valuable lessons to be learned from the world's response and our individual responses. We will remember this virus and the reactions to it for as long as we live. It seemed to be the only thing we heard about for a long time. People were scared. Millions of people were working from home while millions of others lost their jobs. Small business owners struggled to keep their businesses afloat. Others permanently closed and lost everything they had worked hard to build. Many didn't know where their next meal would come from, or how they would pay their rent or mortgage. Schools were closed, and some students transitioned to virtual learning. Parents were worried about their children's education and mental health. Athletes were denied competition when sporting events were completely shut down. Families were kept away from loved ones and faced limits on how they could bury their dead. Some people drowned in the daily onslaught of information, not knowing what information was accurate. Some people became sick with the virus and had to put up a physical fight to survive. Others lost their fight against the virus. The list of hardships could go on and on. For many, it has been an eye-opening period of growth and growing pains. Many of us felt we didn't have many choices. What about you? Did this period help you become more aware, listen more carefully, think more critically for yourself, and choose more wisely?

Recognizing that life is a long series of choices you make for yourself will help you live The Gooder Life. It's easy to fall into a victim mentality of believing you don't have choices. If we believe that, we might blame other people's choices or our current situation instead of taking responsibility for our own choices. You can either accept conditions the way they are or accept responsibility for changing the conditions in your life. I'm not ignoring the fact that there are many things out of our control, but we are always able to choose our attitude and our actions. It is a powerful, life-changing thing when we fully understand the impact of making conscious choices. Letting circumstances dictate our lives will leave us in the "average" lane of life. But looking deeply at our circumstances and realizing that we can change our circumstances by making wise choices will indeed set us apart.

For years now, I've told my children that everyone receives new opportunities at one point or another. The dawn of each day is a new opportunity. Starting a new job and meeting new coworkers is a new opportunity. Starting college is a new opportunity. Simply meeting a new group of people is a new opportunity. In each of those examples, we can decide who we want to be. Do we go in as the person we have always been, or do we take that new opportunity to become the person we have always wanted to be? The power of change is totally ours. Richard Feynman, a renowned theoretical physicist, summed it up well when he said, "You are under no obligation to remain the same person you were a year ago, a month ago, or even a day ago. You are here to create yourself, continuously."

Make a choice and reaffirm that choice each day to live more than a mundane life. That doesn't mean you're constantly going to be doing exciting things. It means you are deciding to do things that will lift you above the crowd and set you apart from everyone else. It means you are striving to be the best you can be in all you do. It means you will choose to be better today than you were yesterday.

Striving to live The Gooder Life means asking ourselves questions about every action in our life. We may not always make the right choices but stopping to consider each choice is a step in the right direction. Each day, you are given a brand-new opportunity. If you are not happy with who you are, you have the power to change YOU by making different choices in life. You don't have to wait; you can start right now. It's up to you. Choose well.

What is a significant choice you can make today?

_____
_____
_____

What do you feel is out of your control?

_____
_____
_____

Remember, you have more control than you think. What is an area that you can control?

_____

_____

_____

FINISH

"Show me a man who cannot bother
to do little things and I'll show you
a man who cannot be trusted to
do big things." Lawrence D. Bell

Let's be honest. Many of us have some project or job that we have not completed. Why is that? If it was important enough to start, why wasn't it important enough to finish? Maybe we took on something beyond our skill set. Maybe it seemed like a fun thing to do before we realized it was not fun at all. Maybe we had too many projects going at once. Whatever the reason, we could avoid some of our unfinished projects if we would think hard before starting them and make better choices for ourselves. If you made a choice to begin something, you must make a choice to finish it.

When we put off a task, it becomes more difficult to get back to finishing it. Procrastination may well be the biggest factor involved in our unfinished business. We are all guilty of it at some time or another. You may not realize if you are a chronic procrastinator, so I suggest asking someone close to you for their perspective. If you habitually procrastinate, you must honestly consider why you do it and make a choice to stop.

One afternoon I was sitting in my work office when I started smelling a terrible burning smell. I got up and started walking around trying to find the smell's origin. My office was on the second floor of the building, and I could not find anything that was causing the awful stench. As I started down the stairs to the first floor, the odor intensified. I was on the right track.

The smell became very strong as I approached the downstairs coffee area. I finally found the problem. Someone had poured the last cup of coffee and put the empty carafe back on the hot burner. The burner had scorched the remaining drops of coffee in the carafe, and the burning smell had permeated the building. I turned off the warmer and put the pot in a place where it could cool down. The pot would have to be cleaned later.

The next afternoon, the odor returned. I immediately rushed downstairs. Once again, someone had left an empty carafe on the hot burner plate. How could they make the same mistake? Again, I turned the burner off and set the pot so it could cool. This time, I went back to my desk and created a sign that said, "Please do not set an empty pot on the hot burner."

But the next day, the same thing happened again. It wasn't a thoughtless act; someone was consciously deciding to take the last cup of coffee and not make another pot. The person responsible was not a finisher. Their actions showed a lack of respect for the rest of us.

One weekend, Kathy and I took a getaway trip to Branson, Missouri. When we arrived in our hotel room, I realized I had forgotten to bring my iPhone charger. After we had eaten supper that evening, we stopped at a Target to purchase a charger. While I was standing in the aisle looking at the iPhone accessories, I overheard a conversation in the next isle over between a dad and his small child. The dad was pushing a shopping cart and the child was riding in it. As they moved down a toy aisle, the child noticed a stuffed animal that had fallen off the shelf and onto the floor. "Look daddy, there's an animal on the floor," the child said. The dad politely acknowledged that there was indeed an animal on the floor. The next part of the conversation is what surprised me. As the dad pushed the cart past the animal, the boy asked, "Aren't we going to put the animal back on the shelf?" The father replied, "No, because we weren't the ones who put it there." This dad was not a finisher.

I have a mentor who has a sign in his office that says, "Leave it better than you found it." That dad in Target who refused to pick up the toy missed a prime teaching moment with his child. He could have taught his boy to leave something better than he found it, but he didn't. Sadly, he taught his son a different lesson altogether. Don Tyson, former CEO and founder of Tyson Foods, would tell his employees, "If you see something that needs to be done and you have the ability to do it, then that is your job." The dad had the ability, but he didn't finish the job.

Kathy and I rented apartments and duplexes before purchasing our first home. We have also rented places to live in between some of our home building projects. Although we were paying to live there, these places didn't actually belong to us.

When we moved out of each of these locations, we could have left the cleaning up to the owners. But it was a priority that we left these rentals in better shape than they were in when we arrived. We wanted to be finishers.

When I borrow something, I always strive to return it better than I found it. If I borrow a car, then I should return it with more fuel in the tank than when I took it. If I borrow a lawn mower, I put gas in it and wash it before I return it. If I borrow a tool, I clean it well before I return it. Give things back better than they were when you took them and return them as soon as possible. That is finishing.

Many retailers have shopping carts available for use at their front door. Those carts are the property of that store. The store is allowing and encouraging customers to borrow the cart for a short period while shopping. They have two purposes for this: it makes shopping convenient for their customers, and they know customers are likely to spend more money if they can carry more.

In 2016, I purchased a new white Ram eco-diesel pickup truck. Not long after that purchase, I went grocery shopping at a large retailer. I came out of the store with my groceries and noticed that a shopping cart had rolled across the parking lot and hit my NEW truck. As I walked toward my vehicle, I could see the dent in the door from a few feet away. I was so disappointed and angry. Why would someone leave their shopping cart out in the lot like that? And how could they let it roll all the way across the lot to hit my truck? This incident started my informal study of shopping carts.

After doing a few internet searches, I found that the shopping cart was invented by Sylvan Goldman, the owner of the "Humpty Dumpty" grocery stores. He rolled out his first cart on June 4th, 1937. That cart was a folding chair with wheels on the legs and a basket sitting on the chair. Up until that point, shoppers had to carry their goods in their arms. Mr. Goldman realized that shoppers could carry more items with a rolling basket, which meant more sales. American ingenuity at its finest. Shopping carts have come a long way since then. It's now a much heavier metal object that can do some damage when it runs into a car (*ahem*: my new truck).

After the incident with my truck, I noticed how many carts were idly sitting all over the lot whenever I went to the grocery store. Most stores provide corrals for shoppers to put their empty carts in, but a significant number of shoppers seemed to ignore them. I began to wonder, "Does a person's behavior with a shopping cart reveal something about them personally?" I realized soon after that, in most cases, it does.

The purpose of the cart is to carry goods that we want to purchase to the check-out location. We can also use the cart to take the purchased items to our vehicles in the parking lot. After we unload our items, the purpose of the cart is complete, but the borrower of that cart still has a job to finish. The store has allowed us to borrow the cart. The least we can do is put the cart in the corral. This will allow an employee to come out and easily round up all the carts later. If we do not take the cart to the corral, then we are leaving our job unfinished.

Someone else will have to complete our job later. We are also disrespecting the cart's owner if we leave out a stray cart. And we are disrespecting the owners of parked vehicles in the lot.

Which type of person are you? Do you respectfully put your shopping cart in the corral? Or do you leave it in the lot to aimlessly roll into vehicles, like the one that rolled into my truck? Are you the person who pours the last cup of coffee and puts the empty pot back on the hot burner? Do you do this knowing that it will burn the last drips of coffee, and someone else will have to clean up your mess? Or are you the person that realizes the pot is empty and takes the time to finish the job and make another pot?

We all have a choice. We can *almost* finish the job or *completely* finish the job. The word responsibility is made up of two words: response and ability. You have the ability to put the shopping cart where it belongs. What will your response be? You have the ability to make another pot of coffee. What will your response be? You have the ability to pick up the stuffed toy that has fallen on the floor in the aisle. What will your response be? Will you be a responsible finisher?

These examples are about small matters. But if you make it your habit to finish the small things, you will be trusted to finish the bigger things. Your manager and co-workers are probably aware of how well you complete your duties and assignments. Be sure they know you can be trusted with finishing all things, big and small. People who get things done get ahead.

Since I received the ugly dent in my truck and became more aware of shopping carts and those who use them, I have learned a few good lessons:

- When someone allows you to borrow something, treat the item with respect and return it better than you found it.

- Be thankful that you can borrow something that makes your life easier.

- When you are doing any job, don't stop short of completion. Finish the job.

I have told this shopping cart example to many individuals and groups of people over the last few years. The phrase "put your shopping cart away" has now become an all-encompassing phrase translating to "finish the job."

A friend of mine was mowing his yard one Saturday afternoon. It was the middle of summer, and the day was hot and very humid. After the mowing was complete, my friend sat down to have a drink of water and cool off for a while. He looked out over the yard knowing that he still had to complete the trimming, then blow off the clippings from the sidewalk and driveway. He told me that he was going to wait until the next day to finish up those last tasks. But then he remembered the saying, "put your shopping cart away." He realized he needed to finish the job right then.

Imagine what your workplace would be like if every employee finished every task and did not procrastinate on a single item. Your company would most definitely be efficient and successful. That may be wishful thinking, but it can start with you. In other words: *put your shopping cart away!*

Are you a procrastinator? Why?

_____
_____
_____

What keeps you from finishing?

_____
_____
_____

What was the last thing you finished?

_____
_____
_____

What is the most important thing you can do to be a better finisher?

_____
_____
_____

CONCLUSION

Urban Dictionary defines "long game" as, "Considering the future implications of current choices, thinking ahead, being deliberate and patient." The Gooder Life is a long game. You've likely heard the phrase, "Don't lose sight of the forest for the trees." Stephen Covey expresses it another way, "Don't be buried in the thick of the thin things." The meaning of these phrases is to not get so caught up in the details that you forget to look at the big picture. Don't let your purpose become blurred by potentially distracting details. If you do, you might not be able to live your life to the fullest. Details are important, but you must also remember that The Gooder Life doesn't come about in a single day. It's an attitude change. A perspective change. A long game.

Living The Gooder Life helps you focus on being better today than you were yesterday. There will be days when moving ahead is hard. There will be days when you feel that you have gone backwards. It's okay—tomorrow will come and you will have another chance to be better.

I love the 2016 Kia Sorento TV commercial where a young boy receives a trophy after a football game. When his father looks at the trophy, he notices that it is a participation trophy. We hear his inner dialogue, which questions why his son was given a participation trophy even though his team won all their games. They didn't just participate; they were the champs. The father proceeds to peel the participation sticker off the front of the trophy. Then, using a Sharpie, he writes "CHAMPS" on the trophy. Finally, he hands the trophy to his son and says, "Here you go, champ." In the real world there are winners and losers. Winners put in the extra work. They make a choice to be the best version of themselves. They are not satisfied with the status quo.

The goal of The Gooder Life is to live a deeper, more fulfilling existence that will set you apart from the crowd. Unfortunately, most people are just happy with getting by. In school, from elementary through college, some try to pass a class instead of striving for an "A" and a position at the top of the class. Employees may be content to have a job and receive a paycheck instead of setting their sights on being the best worker in their group or the leader of the group. The world is sending out a message that being okay is good enough, that being standard is just right. My wife calls this "excelling at mediocrity." We need people who are not content with mediocrity. We need people who want to be the best, people who don't want a participation trophy but instead want the winner's trophy. We need people who are not satisfied with being followers, but who strive to be leaders. We only have one life to live—so why not set out to be the absolute best we can be?

As I have grown older and learned how to live a more fulfilling life, I have come to understand that living a Gooder Life is sometimes tiring. It is hard at times. It is rewarding at times. It is sometimes tedious. But above all else, it is worthwhile.

Living with The Gooder Life principles will help you come to your own understanding of what your purpose is. It will give you direction no matter your circumstances. The Gooder Life will give you the ability to navigate obstacles because you will have trained yourself to be aware of them. You will take the time to think about what you should do and make a choice as to how you will cope with obstacles, all while staying on track for your purpose. Living The Gooder Life helps you be more aware and be a better thinker so you can dig below the everyday layers and meanings of life to unearth deeper layers of truth. Once there, you can contemplate what life is really about for you. The world often seems like it is a big movie with people just going through the motions. Each day, these people aren't sure why they are doing what they are doing. If you are living The Gooder Life, you won't be satisfied just going through the motions. You'll want more out of life. You'll want more out of your relationships. You'll want more out of you. You will begin to learn why you are doing what you are doing each day.

The Gooder Life is the compass that points us in the right direction. It becomes the filter through which we view life. It is the standard by which we measure all things. It is our guide to a more meaningful and successful life.

IN MEMORY OF BECKY

It's odd to think that the loss of Becky carried me on a journey toward The Gooder Life. The questions that have no answers, the determination to continue living my life, the change in how I thought about almost every aspect of life, the drive to move forward—all of that was sparked by her death. I am filled with gratitude that my relationship with Becky was great for the years we had together. Her life and her absence are always with me, and she is a large part of what made this book possible. I will love her forever.

CPSIA information can be obtained
at www.ICGtesting.com
Printed in the USA
JSHW040531020222
22500JS00002B/9